Goe

# Goetic Demons

### New Theories on Demonic Magick

*by Lucien Rofocale*

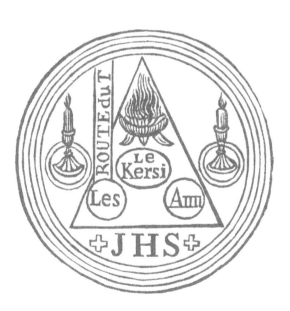

**Dark Moon Press ❖ Fort Wayne, IN**

*Goetic Demons*

*Goetic Demons* ISBN-13: 978-1466335295 \
2011 by Lucien Rofocale and Dark Moon Press

Published by Dark Moon Press
PO Box 11496, Fort Wayne, IN 46858

# Table of Contents

*Goetic Demons*

# 𝕴𝖓𝖙𝖗𝖔𝖉𝖚𝖈𝖙𝖎𝖔𝖓

Everyone seems to think they know about demons, from either a Judeo-Christian point of view or from watching movie with evil creatures in them from *The Prophecy* movies to *Charmed*, but once you actually become truly interested in learning about them from a academic curiosity you find out then how little you know as I did. Lucien Rofocale's exploration into demonology, especially the Goetic demons is one such volume needed in any Gnostic or occultist library as is *Necromancy: the forbidden Art*, also from Dark Moon Press.

The history of demonology, the stories of the Bibles King Solomon, and how to work with demons is covered here as well as a useful listing of both Goetic and Sumerian demons if you wish to follow up on the subject in more depth. Tread cautiously my reader, for you are about to be amazed, educated and enthralled as you turn these pages.

Corvis Nocturnum

*Goetic Demons*

# Chapter One

# Revisioning the Goetia

There is a much misunderstood order of entities which exist on the spiritual or astral plane. They have been described as both angels and demons by those who have encountered them in their occult explorations. Metaphysicians have been aware of such beings for thousands of years, and their interactions with humanity have been recorded in a wide range of literature, from oral tradition, to myth, legend, and even scripture.

Superficially, these beings are known as demons. And yet our modern understanding of that word barely encompasses what these entities really are. The modern conception of demons is completely intertwined with Judeo-Christian beliefs in damnation and redemption, Heaven and Hell, and an ancient, bitter Angel War that led to the expulsion of a third of the angels from Heaven – and the founding of an antithetical order of beings out to decimate humanity through torment and temptation.

But what are demons really? Regardless of beliefs in Heaven or Hell, demons are typically seen as creatures that inhabit another realm. This realm separate from and yet contiguous with our own –

as proved by the tremendous amount of traffic carried out by the demons between the two realms. This much is certainly true.

In medieval writings, while some demons were seen as literal flesh and blood creatures, capable of having sex with mortals, as in the case of incubus and succubus demons, many were described as possessing "aeriel" bodies -- that is to say, bodies that are physical but just barely. They have subtle flesh that is malleable and permeable in ways that air is, but not generally more physical things like human flesh. This idea of the "airy" composition of demon bodies was propagated by religious scholars, such as Father Lodovico Sinistrari, author of the text *Demoniality*. In part, this belief was developed in order to explain away some of the powers of demons: that they could enter locked buildings, float through windows and walls, travel great distances invisibly, and move almost instantaneously from one place to another with a mere flexing of their will.

*Medieval depiction of the Devil*

Although some of the demons of the Middle Ages were thought to interact in an almost sympathetic fashion with human beings (Sinistrari tells of one incubus that fell in love with a mortal woman and spent years trying to woo her. He almost never attacked her, but instead just moped about like a moonstruck teenager), demons are generally seen as antagonistic toward humanity. The bulk of their number are typified as being bent on the destruction, torment, and torture of human beings. Not all demons were believed to be wholly evil, however. Some were ambivalent toward humanity, while others could even be coerced into helping people. In fact, in Middle Ages and Renaissance Europe, there flourished a tradition that demons could be bent to the will of mortals and forced into a kind of magickal servitude. This belief had its roots in beliefs and practices from the Hellenic world, which in turn were influenced by traditions older still.

The very word "demon" comes from the Greek *daimones,* and this word had fairly complex associations in the ancient world. Greek daimons were not wholly evil entities. They were otherworldly, to be sure, and they existed in a space a step above humanity but also a step below the gods. As such, they often served as intermediaries and messengers between humanity and the gods. They were, on the whole, neutral creatures. Some were essentially good, and the Greeks called these *eudaimones.* Others were essentially bad, and the Greeks called these *cacodaimones.* Of course, the good and evil of the eudaimons and the cacodaimons was not cut and dried. To say that

9

the eudaimons were good was not to imply that they were all sugar and rainbows, peace and love. No, the Greek understanding of these beings is that they would work to guide humanity to be in balance with their souls. They were beings of order and they helped humanity to better fit into the cosmic order, including helping people to better follow their individual paths.

The cacodaimons were more about chaos. They sought to drive people into imbalance, and thus to throw the order out of whack. Their evil is not the kind of black and white evil that average people tend to conceive today. They were spirit guides – but in the worst sense, for they sought always to thwart the balanced and wholesome growth of the individual.

The belief in daimons in the Classical world was widespread. The philosopher Socrates rather famously was guided by a daimon, which functioned as his good genius right up until the end. In a fairly famous speech, allegedly made before the Athenians just prior to his execution, Socrates observed that his death could not be a bad thing, because his guiding daimon had always stayed his hand before he did something ill advised, and that morning, it had nothing to say. So Socrates drank the poison hemlock, content with his fate.

Of course, the concept of daimons changed significantly in the hands of the Church. Early Christianity had already established a starkly dualistic view of the world, and the hosts of Heaven were, in their opinion, locked in immortal, spiritual combat with the hosts of Hell. Satan, Belial, Beelzebub, and Lucifer were all major players in this struggle, and they pitted themselves against the armies of God and its most charismatic leaders: the Son of God and the Archangel Michael, the leader of the armies of the Lord.

I could go on and on about how early Christian notions practically invented the notion of hell, damnation, and the devil, but suffice it to say that the nature of these entities is highly controversial, primarily because it is tied up so thoroughly in the Western imagination with ancient religious tradition. Thus far, however, few magickal workers have undertaken a serious attempt to explore or understand these entities primarily because of the taboos created by that religious tradition. Unfortunately, the few modern works extant on the subject have been the product of those with an unhealthy attraction to the subject precisely because of the taboos. It can be clearly seen that despite the fact that most magickal workers stem from a religious background that has broken away from the Biblical faiths, the superstitious dread still holds.

Prince Bael, from de Plancy's *Dictionnaire Infernal*

Just as we in the modern era have exploded the myth that all witches make a pact with the devil for their powers and keep demons as their familiars, so too should we attempt to explode the myths surrounding those entities believed to be demons. There exists a long and oft-neglected Western tradition which addresses the nature of these beings and their potential to interact with and be directed by humanity. This tradition stems primarily from the Solomonic tradition of the Old Testament as well as a number of extra-Biblical texts, most notably the text known as *The Clavicle of Solomon* and the *Goetia*.

# Chapter Two

# The Roots of Demonology

T he roots of modern demonology stretch back to the Solomonic tradition of the Old Testament. Most existing texts on Goetic evocation are derived from one primary source: the Clavicle of Solomon. This text, which according to tradition was written by King Solomon himself, gives modern demonology its biblical and essentially Hebraic character. As this is the primary text from which all other texts are derived, no inquiry into the nature of demonology can adequately begin without a careful analysis of the Solomonic tradition.

King Solomon, son of David, appears in the book of Kings one, chapters 1 through 11, the some details concerning the circumstances of Solomon's birth appear in the second book of Samuel. According to biblical tradition, Solomon was the youngest son of King David, child of his wife Bathsheba. Bathsheba it should be noted was a wife whom David procured through rather scandalous and treacherous circumstances. Salomon is described as being a boy when his father David dies, and though there is some dispute to his reign at first, this is quickly settled, and Solomon takes the throne unopposed.

Biblical tradition characterizes Solomon as the wisest of old kings to reign over the people of Israel. Here is how it happened: Solomon was praying and the Lord God appeared to him. God asked to Solomon what gift he would wish as successor to King David's throne. Solomon, clearly a young man uncertain of his capacity to rule such a nation as that of the Israelites, and in awe of his famous father, first praises David's greatest strengths to his God, focusing on David's overwhelming gentleness and kindness. He then decides that if God were to grant him anything, it would have to be a wise heart so that he may fairly judge and lead his great nation of people.

God is well pleased with this humble request. It befits a ruler to desire more for his people than for himself. God then tells Solomon that because he did not ask for riches, or a long life, or the conquest of his enemies, but instead merely wisdom, God would grant to Solomon not only wisdom but all of these other things. For so long as Solomon upheld the laws of his God and did not worship other gods before him, the Lord God would make Solomon the wisest of all rulers to walk the earth. And never before nor ever again would any man be as great a ruler of Solomon and were as wise. With promises of peace, prosperity, and something of a golden age for the Israelites, God's presence departs.

Thus (according to the story) a Solomon became the wisest of men, and for his great wisdom and careful rule, all men saw that the grace of the Lord God shone upon Solomon his servant as it had for David his father before him.

It is during the reign of King Solomon that the great temple of the Israelites is built. A good deal of Kings I in the Bible is devoted to the construction of this temple, its design, the materials used to build it, and its cost to the nation of Israel. A good deal of occult lore has grown up around this temple which God promises will represent the glory of the nation of Israel until or unless that nation displeases him and he will cause it to be torn down.

Significantly, both the masons and the Knights Templar traced much of their esoteric heritage to the building of the temple. The Knights Templar were so named because they establish themselves in Jerusalem on what was believed to be the site of the temple before it finally fell before the Romans. The Masonic symbology in toto is derived from those passages in Kings one as well as an extra-biblical text by Josephus detailing the construction of the temple and the significance of its design and decoration.

*Guardian figure from the palace at Ashurbanipal*

Although no direct mention of demons is made in Kings one, a strong extra-biblical tradition exists which links the construction of the temple to demonology directly through the person of Solomon the King.

The Testament of Solomon, which alleges to have been written by King Solomon himself, describes the circumstances which led to King Solomon being given power over all demonkind by Lord God. There are some problems with the attribution that Solomon wrote this Testament however. There are numerous passages within the text that suggest that it was actually written, or at the very least rewritten, after the dawn of Christianity. A number of passages foreshadow the birth of Christ, for example, citing details connected with the Savior that were not established in Solomon's time. Current scholars date the work to the Hellenic period. The work, written in Greek, was almost certainly produced within the first three centuries

16

of the Christian era. There is every likelihood that the book is based upon an older tradition still, but the version that has survived the test of time is only a little under 2000 years old. The author is unknown, but, despite how it is presented in the text, the version we have today was not written by Solomon himself.

Whatever the true source of the Testament of Solomon, in medieval times it was accepted as the true writings of Solomon himself. It is from this Testament that medieval demonology derives notions such as the Seal of Solomon as well as Solomon's Brazen Vessel.

*Goetic Demons*

# Chapter Three
# King Solomon

olomon's reign is the beginning of a golden age for the Israelites. It is under Solomon that the famous temple which housed the ark of the covenant was built. Both the Old Testament and the writings of the extra-Biblical historian Josephus document the building of this lavish temple. Most students of the occult have at one time or another come across references to this temple, as its construction and symbolism serve as the foundation for aspects of both the Knights Templar and the Order of Freemasons. The temple also plays a role in the extra-Biblical goetic tradition.

According to the Testament of Solomon, the king had more than mortal help in the building of his temple. Apparently, as Solomon was favored by the Old Testament god, that god saw fit to give Solomon a seal, set in a ring, which would give the king of the Israelites power over demons and the angels that had been cast from heaven. Solomon wasted no time in putting this ring to good use, first rescuing the son of a favored worker from the nightly predations of a local demon known as Ornias. After that demon had been commanded to give up the names and locations of a number of its brethren, Solomon set to work summoning, questioning, and then binding every demonic entity he could get his hands on. The Testament of Solomon enumerates each and every one of these bindings, listing the names of the demons, their particular powers and weaknesses, and the magickal names – usually those of angels, but sometimes secret names of God – that bind and compel them.

Though a wise and just king as far as the Israelites were concerned, Solomon, by his own testament, was rather ruthless and without mercy when it came to demonkind. With most of these demons, he extorted what information he could from them, threatening them with the seal given him by his god as well as with the retribution of that god if they did not yield to Solomon's power.

*The Seal of Solomon*

He used one of the demons to locate mines of precious gems and ores, and these were to become the famous mines of Solomon.

Others he bound up in bottles and similar vessels, but still others he ordered to work on the temple in arduous tasks, such as moving huge blocks of stone that his mortal workers could not manage. One female demon he bound to the gates of the temple so that all could see that he had captured her and subdued her.

The testament of Solomon has clearly been rewritten a number of times, and in that time, has inevitably suffered from isegesis. Most notable is the insertion of references to Christ as the Messiah and the greatest of the "angels" who the demons fear and hate. Nevertheless, the demonic tradition described in the testament is pre-Christian, and though the writer was not likely Solomon himself, it seems clear that the writer was attempting to describe the system of goetic philosophy attributed to Solomon. The demons introduced through the testament each have a sphere of influence which they hold power over, as well as a specific angel whose name can drive them away. In at least a few cases, the name of the angel that holds power over a given demon is directly stated as the name of that demon's *father*. This is a powerful subtext that exists within the *Testament of Solomon*. Several of the demons claim to be the offspring of angels. At least one claims to be an angel himself who came down and sired demonic children of his own. This is a concept that goes back to fragmentary lines in the Biblical Book of Genesis as well as the near-mythic *Book of Enoch*. In the Enochian tradition, a group of angels, called the *Grigori* or Watchers, left Heaven of their own accord. They gathered on the slopes of Mount Hermon and swore to

21

join humanity and take wives for themselves. Their leaders are variously identified as Shemyaza, Azazel and, in a later chapter in *Enoch I,* Jequon. Regardless of the name of the leader, the important part of the tale is that these angels left, mated with humanity, and had children of their own. The children were neither human nor angel, but a blending of both. The *Book of Enoch* calls them *Nephilim,* and this word is retained in the Old Testament books of the Bible, appearing again and again – often without much useful context. The offspring of these rebel angels were also called variously Gibborim (giants) and Rephaim (heroes – it came to mean the heroic dead). Their angelic fathers taught forbidden knowledge to humanity, including enchantments, weapon-making, root-cutting, astrology, and even abortion (described in the text as the "smiting of the infant in the womb).

*Gustav Doré's Satan cast from Heaven*

The demons of the *Testament of Solomon* are the direct inheritors of this belief in the Nephilim, and notably, the *Book of Enoch* was set down some time in the last few centuries just prior to the Christian era – although the references in Genesis to the Watchers' tale suggests that the story itself is much older still. All of the stories surrounding the mating of angels with human wives and their subsequent inhuman offspring suggests that the line between demons and angels is a thin one indeed. Quite notably, throughout the Middle Ages, the was a persistent belief that the demons that haunted humanity, tormenting people through temptation and disease, were in fact the restless ghosts of the children of the Watchers – inhuman spirits killed by a vengeful God, unable to live in the world but also unable to leave.

# Chapter Four

# Angels and Demons

The Hebraic system which gave rise to the Old Testament had a complex tradition of angelology. Angels were believed to have been created before man but after substance was brought out of the void. They were immortal, ethereal, and androgyne, and were believed to exist on a spiritual level just above mankind. Some angels were primarily good, such as the archangels who represented the four elements, and these served the function of guardians and warriors for the Hebrew god (hence their designation as "heavenly hosts" -- host in the sense of a standing army). Some angels were of a darker nature, such as the Adversary (*shaitan*) and the Angel of Death (*Malach ha-Mavet*), and these were used by the Hebrew god to plague and test humanity. Despite their adversarial position to humanity, however, it is important to note that these entities, even the Adversary, who gave rise to the Christian devil, are depicted as residing in the heaven of the Hebrew god alongside their angelic counterparts. Furthermore, "bad" angels or "good", all took orders from the god of the Old Testament.

As the tradition has come down to us, those beings whose functions were lighter and more positive were termed angels. Those whose functions were darker were termed demons. In the Shemhamphorash, these are distinguished as angels of mercy versus angels of judgment. Angels of mercy are the thirty-six of seventy-two names ending in the suffix

–iah. The angels of judgment have names ending in –iel. As ceremonial magick developed over the years, these seventy-two entities became irrevocably connected with another seventy-two demons, but the fact of the matter is that the demons are already there in the Shemhamphorash. They are the angels of judgment, associated with night and existing in equal opposition of power to the good-natured angels of mercy. This is the fallacy of demonic magick fed to practitioners these days. There are no demons that are not also angels. They are all otherworldly beings that exist upon the spiritual hierarchy somewhere in a space above humanity yet below any god.

Of course, as Christianity was rooted in the Hebraic tradition, it inherited a strong belief in these entities. However, Christianity is far more dualistic in its outlook than the Hebraic system, as it borrows heavily also from Zoroastrianism. As a result, Christianity envisioned a stark dichotomy between the angels and demons, depicting the angels are wholly good servants of the creator and making demons into the wholly evil adversaries of that creator.

With the rise of the Catholic Church and its subsequent Inquisitions, this distinction has grown even more stark and more severe, until demons have become the absolute embodiment of evil and are believed to strike out at the creator constantly and insidiously. Especially in the social climate of the witchtrials, inquisitors needed a foul creature that was inarguably corrupt and evil to associate with a target in order to completely destroy that target's public reputation. Inquisitors styled demons into a force which best served their political agenda. Accordingly, the propaganda of the Inquisition made it the favorite pastime of demons to lead mankind astray. If this were not the case, how else could they justify the involvement of demons in the affairs of mortals and the subsequent charges that damned thousands to the flames? The fanaticism which is encouraged by these beliefs makes it very difficult to gain an objective, unbiased view of that class of beings which the Hebraic system was attempting to describe.

*Woodcut of a Seraphim*

Though it is nearly impossible to get a clear picture of what an angel or a demon truly is without a couple thousand years' worth of dogma getting in the way, the occurrence of similar entities in other major world religions seems to suggest that there is something real to be found underneath the many layers of mythologized tradition. In Hindu mythology, there are asuras and devas which equate to demons and angels, respectively, and these beings also occupy an ambivalent spiritual place somewhere between good and evil, mankind and the gods. The Buddhist system, too, has entities which occupy this neither human nor fully divine place in the spiritual hierarchy. In the West, a tradition has come down to us which purports to address the nature of these beings, though even these texts have been infected by the Hebraic and Christian traditions to some extent. The tradition is called the *Goetia*, and it deals primarily with the evocation of spirits.

# Chapter Five

# The Goetic Tradition

T he *Goetia* is the Western system of magick which arose from the Solomonic tradition. The *Goetia* is based upon the premise that angels and demons are subservient to the Hebraic god and that by invoking them with the sacred names of this god, the industrious magickal worker can command these beings, discourse with them, curry favors, and extort knowledge from them. The *Goetia* shows evidence of influence from Greek and Roman sources, particularly the curse tablets known as *defixiones*. The term "goetia" itself is derives from the Greek word *goês*, to groan or lament (as in lamenting the dead). There is an implication of a shamanic system with early Goetic magick, as the practitioner often serves as an intermediary between the realm of the living and the realm of the dead. Once the Goetia spills into ceremonial magick, however, it becomes fused with the Qabbalistic tradition and both of these show lingering traces of ancient Assyro-Babylonian magick.

Each angel and each demon is assigned a magickal name, which contains their essential nature, and which, through the Hebraic system of gematria, is reducible to a number. The angels and demons each have a corresponding position in the Sephiroth, or Tree of Life (in the case of the demons, this is more properly called the Qlipphoth, the dark reflection of the Tree of Life). Each has a position in the angelic / demonic hierarchy. This hierarchy is based on a monarchial system, and each level is further equated with a celestial sphere. The Earls are associated with Mars, the Dukes with Venus, the Marquis with the Moon, Presidents with Mercury, Princes with Jupiter, and Kings with the Sun. Each demon is also assigned a sign of the Zodiac as well as a time of the day.

The angels and demons are both arranged in Orders. Archangels, Seraphim, and Cherubim seem particular only to angels, however both angels and demons share a number of other orders. There are the Orders of Thrones, Powers, Dominions, Virtues, Principalities, and Angels (to which belong both angels and demons). As the Hebraic system recognizes the angels as primarily the servants of YHWH, only the demons, who are somewhat ambiguous in their allegiance, are described as the subjects of summonings and bindings. Occasionally, there is confusion on this point, as there is an angelic tradition of magick that seeks to call upon the powers of the mighty hosts still loyal to YHWH. Angelic sigils do appear in a number of other similar magickal texts from the same time period. However, the *Goetia* contains a very specific set of sigils that are intended to connect with goetic entities only. The main purpose of the *Goetia* is to describe the essential appearance of a number of demons, their place in demonic hierarchy, and their powers. The names and sigils which can summon and bind them are also provided, as is an extensive and exhaustive system of ceremonial magick through which one can supposedly evoke these beings.

Experiments with the *Goetia* demonstrate that there are a number of entities which occupy the spiritual place traditionally assigned to angels and demons. I hesitate to term these beings either angels or demons because of the heavy religious connotations which accompany either of those terms. Some, though not all, of the sigils and names attributed to these beings resonate with them, so much so that they may adequately be used to call them. The traditional powers assigned to each of these beings in most cases seem to hold true. They seem for the most part to be spiritual identities, almost in the mathematical sense of the word. It is interesting to note that the names of these beings, according to *Goetic* tradition, can be reduced to a number rather like an equation. Many of their sigils, as well, seem designed on mathematical principles, utilizing both geometry and trigonometry. The best results are gained when these mathematical systems are applied to the sigils. They should be approached almost as formulae, patterns that resonate with a specific energy and attract whatever being resonates with the same.

# Chapter Six

# Working with the Demons

raditionally, the beings described in the *Goetia* are only summoned after a long period of preparation on the part of the magickal worker. All effort is made to insure that the magickal worker is purified, and even then, he goes to the summoning armed with a number of weapons and items designed to protect him from the malignant force of the entity he intends upon summoning. A complex summoning circle is constructed into which the entity is to be evoked, while an equally complex circle of protection is constructed for the magickal worker to operate from. All of this seems a bit melodramatic and overdone in the light that the goetic entities are, in all likelihood, not infernal representatives of the nether realm out to divest the magickal worker of his immortal soul. As simply another order of spiritual entities whose existence lies predominantly on the astral or subtle reality, most of the precautions used when dealing with them are unnecessary and based upon the spiritual prejudices put forward by Christianity.

Like all spiritual entities, work with the goetic beings should be undertaken only by those who are confident in their ability to perceive, understand, and interact with the spiritual level of reality. Wiccans and neo-Pagans who have looked upon the *Goetia* with a kind of superstitious dread should rethink their cosmologies. If there is no Satan and there is no Hell as traditionally defined by the Church, how can there be traditional demons? The answer is simply that there aren't. There are beings that have been called demons, truly. They are beings that have been mistaken for demons. Some of them may seem overwhelmingly dark, but dark is a far cry from infernal. A certain spiritual prejudice has prevented most magickal workers from an objective examination of the information contained in the *Goetia*, but if that prejudice is laid aside, it becomes clear that there is useful information to be gleaned from a careful reading of "demonic" manuscripts.

It is clear that much about the goetic entities has been misunderstood. To think of them as infernal agents out to devour souls is absurd. Good and evil, as they are traditionally understood, are irrelevant terms where these beings are concerned, though it can be said that some are more positive in their powers and some more negative. Even then, however, the entities are as mercurial and as difficult to define as the fey, for just as one demon may "cause wounds from arrows to putrefy" he is also as likely to "teach all things relating to science and the arts." Like any tool, it depends on the use it is put to.

*Goetic Demons*

A number of the goetic entities whose natures are encapsulated in these formulaic sigils seem to be actual beings that exist on some level of the astral plane. In this respect, they are spirits, but they are spirits that have never incarnated among humanity. They never had a human existence and they are completely unable to obtain one through any natural method of physical incarnation.

Where they come from is a mystery. IT is entirely possible that they are indeed Qlipphotic beings in the traditional sense: left-over shells of an earlier creation, still tied to this realm for some reason, and yet nevertheless apart from it. Perhaps the medieval folktales are correct and they are the ghosts of dead angels, haunting the mortal realm. Certainly, they are something wholly other than humanity, and that otherness comes forth in any of their dealings. For those individuals with finely honed psychic senses, these beings are immediately recognizable. Once one has been encountered, their very otherness, that peculiar vibration of their being, is unmistakable.

Like the eudaimons and cacodaimons of ancient Greece, it is foolish to attribute to them standard notions of good and evil. They are neutral beings, although their very alien nature insures that many of their motives may seem evil or destructive sheerly from the fact that they do not quite understand our living realm and its rules. Death has little meaning to them, and this is how several of these beings can easily bring about the death of others, and yet remain in a neutral state, rather than one of strict malevolence. Destruction and harm are simply actions that they can take. As they are disconnected from our world of the flesh, so too are they disconnected from the sense of action of consequence. They have about all of the moral accountability of a handgun – and just as much moral sense. They exist apart from our understanding of good and evil, righteousness and malevolence. Keep this in mind in all of your dealings with them, for it may help you to understand the utter glee with which one of these entities may embark upon a mission of destruction and even empathize with the individual they have been sent to attack while at the very same time carrying out their instructions of vengeance.

In body, they seem to be of a form and substance that precludes incarnation into the physical plane entirely, but psychologically, they are also disconnected from our realm. If it is possible, both their "bodies" and their "spirits" are what keep them from a greater involvement in our world. They simply cannot connect save through extraordinary means, Of course, Goetic magick, when properly performed, constitutes extraordinary means.

Their disconnected and alien nature is certainly part of the reason that these beings are attracted to invocation. While their own nature is too refined to interface adequately with this world on its own, with the insertion of some medium – living or otherwise -- or the construction of a gate, they can connect at least energetically to this realm. The nature of these beings, as it is described in the *Clavicle* and other writings, depicts them as spirits who nevertheless have fairly earthly appetites and desires. They cannot take up flesh. The exist forever apart from it. And yet they are witness to it at all times.

Their realm intersects with ours so intimately that they cannot help but observe us – albeit from a distance that is just significant enough to prevent them from crossing over even as primarily spirit entities without some form of magickal assistance. And they long to connect. They are drawn to powerful emotion and potent experiences because, in drifting in that null space between realities, they have very little of this of their own. They want to touch and taste and see and feel – and the promise of this, far more than any other sacrifice or bargain you can strike with them – will prove worthy coin to exchange for their services. Allowing a Goetic to cross closer to the realm of flesh through a gate constructed of its name and sigil is one way to entice the being and pay it back for services rendered. For more valuable to these beings is the opportunity to ride another's mortal coil.

In ancient manuscripts such as the Leyden Papyrus, this technique involved a young boy or girl – frequently a virgin. The virginity is less important (considering the wholly carnal appetites of some of these demons) than the vulnerability. The medium used by the magus in these interactions needed to be open in mind and spirit. They needed to have few developed defenses to prevent their use as a vessel. In these modern times, the use of any individual under the age of eighteen is inadvisable, but consider instead the utility of individuals with poorly developed emotional boundaries. This is really the key factor involved in such mediumship – assuming it is to be forced. But better than forcing it, giving the demon a willing vessel which it can ride for a set period of time – this will accomplish even more in terms of establishing a relationship with the entity in question.

In all of the ancient manuscripts, the vessel whose flesh is exchanged with the demon and used to allow its manifestation is not that of the magician himself. It is inadvisable to attempt such an arrangement during the first few interactions with these beings. Instead, the magician should build up a relationship with a particular demon. Get to know its personality, needs, and behavior. It is possible to make arrangements for controlled possessory states, but this should only be explored as an option once you are very, very certain of the nature of the being you are dealing with. Goetic spirits will keep their word, if such is formally demanded of them. Oaths are as binding to them as any magickal circle, especially if those oaths are sworn upon their own true Name. But they are also very literal beings – in addition to being tricky. Be wary of the letter of the oath, keeping in mind its strict literal interpretation rather than assuming that the being will uphold the spirit of its promise. In this respect, dealing with goetics is very similar to those legendary interactions between Faustian magicians and their Mephistophiles.

*Goetic Demons*

## Chapter Seven

# What Answers the Call

If we take all of the previous considerations to their logical conclusion, we see that at least some of the entities we know as goetics are spirits which, although they cannot connect to the earthly realm of their own accord, nevertheless have a desire to connect with and thereby experience this realm. As they seem to need a human medium to clear the way for this connection, the entire tradition of invocation and evocation suddenly makes a great deal of sense. Spirits with a desire to interact with this realm, and yet lacking the capacity for such within themselves, might gladly share some knowledge, skill, or ability in exchange for the opportunity to connect via a human medium.

Not all of the sigils are accurate representations of the formula which they may have originally been intended to record. Grimoires in the Middle Ages were hand written, copied from one magickal practitioner to another. Such copies were frequently made in secret, and one can assume that a sense of urgency, coupled with a fear of being caught, may have inspired at least one rushed job. With the scribe's hand shaking and his attention wandering every few moments to the door, one can hardly expect absolute accuracy, especially considering the standard margin of human error.

Under such circumstances, and with no set standard publicly known, copyist errors are common, and in the case of several sigils, there is a great discrepancy in both the names and the forms that have come down to us. The demon Leriakhe alone has spellings for his name that vary between Leraie, Leraje, and Leraiel – with no possible way to know which of these variations is the original, as almost all of the known grimoires are copies of copies, with their originals almost certainly long ago burned.

The fanciful scribbles and whorls of a number of the sigils, like that of Beleth or Agares, stand in stark contrast to the elegant and almost mathematical symmetry of signs such as those for Marbas and Sitri. It is the opinion of this author that these asymmetrical sigils have been either embellished, and therefore had their true meaning wrecked, or they were copied completely wrong at some point along the way, the mistake being enlarged upon with each successive recopying. Notably, very few of these asymmetrical sigils seem to successively conjure anything. If one likens goetic sigils to the phone numbers of respective spirits, these miscopied sigils are nothing more or less than wrong numbers. They consistently yield bad connections or, in one or two cases, they direct the magickal worker to an energy that is both unexpected and undesirable.

So, entities of the first sort are legitimate spirits that may seek a symbiotic relationship with the summoner so that they might experience the physical realm. Entities of the second sort are, for all intents and purposes, wrong numbers, and even if something exists on the other end of the call, it is unworkable and undesirable, with energy that is very likely in conflict with the flawed symbol used to call it up.

A woodcarving of Belial from Jacobus de Teramo's book Buche Belial (1473

The sigils of Agares and Beleth, from Collin de Plancy's 1853 *Dictionnaire Infernal*

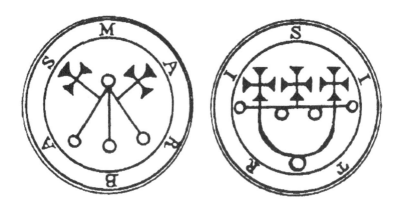

The sigils of Marbas and Sitri, also from de Plancy's *Dictionnaire Infernal*

But there is a third sort of entity that is not strictly a real spirit but it is also not a spiritual wrong number that can lead to undesirable results. This third sort of entity that seems to resonate with the sigils is almost more of a structure than a being. While it adequately performs a specific set of actions, it does some seem to do so with any amount of sentience or free-will. At times, it seems that the energy evoked through the use of the goetic sigil is little more than a spiritual framework or program which defines a set magickal function -- and function here is meant in the strict mathematical sense. Thus, Andromalius could be described as the demon $F(x)$ and Orobas as $G(x)$. The skilled worker can take up such a framework, donning it almost like a ceremonial robe. In this way, the magickal worker's energies $[x]$ become the value which is plugged into the function $[F(x)]$. The resulting invocation of the entity results in something of a spiritual symbiosis, wherein the worker can channel his own energy through the framework and utilize the powers unique to it.

Such an invocation is not to be undertaken lightly, however. The framework can be further explained as an extension of the identity. (This seems very appropriate to our mathematical metaphor, as a function can serve to define identity). As such, it is necessary to caution those eager to attempt such an exercise. As with any other working of a magickal nature, to adopt an extension to one's identity requires a strong will and a strong sense of self. Those who possess a weak self image may find themselves having much difficulty bearing up under the 'spiritual weight' of the extension.

From the *Goetia* and related texts, it is clear that there is an order of spiritual entities which occupy the place assigned to demons. These entities each have a certain sphere of influence specific to them, and each has a certain sigil and Name which resonates with them. There is something archetypal about many of these entities, and as such they can be invoked in the same way any archetype can be invoked. Invocation, though potentially more risky than evocation, is nevertheless a far simpler operation. It is easier to achieve results and despite traditional fears of possession, it is a simple matter for one to assert one's own identity over that which has been invoked and cease the invocation.

Further, evocation may be the wrong way of going about contacting these entities. As spiritual entities, a visible, physical manifestation is unlikely to occur no matter what the circumstances. For many of the beings described in the *Goetia*, just making their presence known beyond the individual, subtle perceptions of the magickal worker could prove too taxing an effort. The primary mistake of goetic workers in the past seems to have been the expectation that demons would physically appear upon evocation as they are luridly described as manifesting in the folklore of Medieval witchcraft (almost all of which was merely propaganda formulated by the Church). The only recent magickal worker of any note who asserts the claim that such an appearance did occur is Aleister Crowley, and he does not specify how many psychoactive drugs he fumigated his ceremonial chamber with in addition to the incense.

*Goetic* work is an ancient tradition that has fallen by the magickal wayside. Because of the heavy religious connotations which the entities have been given by the Catholic church and succeeding generations of Christianity, even devout pagans find themselves a little leery of attempting interaction with them. However, until more serious, modern work is undertaken to explore the realm of the *Goetia*, the old definitions as well as the old prejudices will remain. As it stands now, the *Goetia* is to modern magickal knowledge what the uncharted sections of the old maps used to be: *Here there be Dragons.* When some adventurous soul finally got up enough nerve to actually face the dragons, he found that there weren't any to speak of. There was exciting and at times treacherous new terrain to be explored, but the monsters that were supposed to guard such uncharted territory were merely personifications of that greatest of monsters: the Unknown. And until the unknown becomes the knowable, our mystical maps will still read: *Here there be Demons.*

*Goetic Demons*

## Appendix: The Goetic Demons

There are a total of seventy-two Goetic demons. Their names appear in the *Goetia*, which is the first book of a larger magickal text known as the *Lemegeton* or *Lesser Key of Solomon the King*. The *Lemegeton* dates probably to the seventeenth century, although it is based on works that are much older. Almost all of the demons named in the *Goetia* also appear in the *Discoverie of Witchcraft*, written in 1584 by Reginald Scot. Scot himself got his list of demons from the *Pseudo-monarchia Daemonum,* a rather infamous text compiled by Johannes Weyer in the middle 1600s. Weyer was a student of Cornelius Agrippa, and he compiled his list of demons from a text that he called the *Liber Spirituum Officiorum*. The exact date of the publication of that text is unknown. In all likelihood, it was not a published book so much as a hand-copied manuscript. Several of the names of the Goetic demons vary between texts, and the diligent student will find it helpful to consult all three texts to compare spellings. Of the three texts, only the *Goetia* also presents the sigils of the demons. These geometric figures are essential for the proper invocation and evocation of these entities. It is very likely that Weyer and Scot left out these sigils so as to discourage people from the proper method of summoning the entities.

Scot's book has much longer entries on each of these demons. The list that follows here is significantly abbreviated and should be used as an introductory guide only. Steve Savedow's *Goetic*

*Evocation* can be consulted for further information, should Scot's *Discoverie of Witchcraft* prove difficult to obtain.

Since the nineteenth century, possibly through the works of Eliphas Levi and most definitely through the practices of the Hermetic Society of the Golden Dawn, the seventy-two angels of the Shemhamphorash have been paired with the seventy-two Goetic demons. This is certainly inspired by the tradition established by the *Testament of Solomon,* where each demon declares that there is a particular angel or holy name that commands and compels him. In many of the old grimoires, there are references to the Shemhamphorash, but these references are brief and come with no specific instructions. As many of the grimoires also often left out specific steps for constructing summoning circles and calling up the spirits, it is probable that the true application of the Shemhamphorash was part of an oral tradition surrounding medieval ceremonial magick. In essence, if one had a copy of a grimoire, it was assumed that such an individual already knew the basics of the art. It is certainly important to note that proper measures for protection should be adhered to in this work and, in addition to observing a certain amount of ritual purity in order to fortify both mind and body against the stresses inevitably brought about by contact with these inhuman energies, it is also important to know, before going into things, basic methods of shielding ad psychic self-defense so as to maintain control over the entities. Weak-willed individuals have no business dabbling in Goetic magick, and they do so at the risk of having one of these spirits subsume them in part or whole.

Here follows the abbreviated list of demons:

## Agares

In demonology, according to some authors, Agares (or Agreas as he is sometimes called) is a Duke (or Grand Duke), ruling the eastern zone of Hell, served by 31 legions of demons.

He can make runaways come back, and those who run stand still. He can also cause earthquakes and teaches languages, finding pleasure in teaching immoral expressions. He also has the power to destroy dignities, (both temporal and supernatural) and can brings runaways home safely as well as drive off enemies.

Agares from Collin de Plancy's *Dictionnaire Infernal*, published in 1863.

**Alloces**

Also spelled Alocer or Alloces he  is a demon whose title is Great Duke of Hell, and who has thirty-six legions of demons under his command. He induces people to immorality and teaches arts and all mysteries of the sky.

He appears in the shape of a knight mounted on an enormous horse. His face has a ruddy complexion and burning eyes; and he speaks with great seriousness. He is said to provide good familiars, and to teach astronomy and liberal arts, and instructs the daimon. He is the provider of familiar spirits.

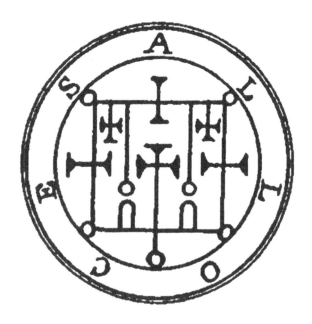

## Amdusias

Also spelled Amduscias and Amdukias) is one of the demons of hell described in the *Goetia*, one of the books of the manuscript grimoire known as the *Lemegeton* or *Lesser Key of Solomon*. He is mentioned by Johann Wierus in his *Pseudomonarchia daemonum*, and by Reginald Scot in *The Discoverie of Witchcraft*. The *Goetia* asserts about this demon:

*"He is a Duke Great and Strong, appearing at first like a Unicorn, but at the request of the Exorcist he standeth before him in Human Shape, causing Trumpets, and all manner of Musical Instruments to be heard, but not soon or immediately. Also he can cause Trees to bend and incline according to the Exorcist's Will. He giveth Excellent Familiars. He governeth 29 Legions of Spirits."*

In Collin de Plancy's illustration, shown with sigil on the next page, Amdusias is crowned to show that he is a duke of hell. He has been given a horse's head to go with his single horn, because unicorns are usually represented in the shape of a horse. Two trumpets lie on the ground, and a third trumpet is slung over his shoulders.

makes trees bend & fall.

(The demon Amdusias from Collin de Plancy's *Dictionnaire Infernal*, 1863)

**Andras**

Andras was the 63rd of the 72 spirits of Solomon and a Grand Marquis of Hell, appearing with a winged angel's body and the head of an owl or raven, riding upon a strong black wolf and wielding a sharp and bright sword. He was also responsible for sowing discord, and commanded 30 infernal legions. He is considered to be a highly dangerous capable of killing the conjuring magician (and his assistants) if precautions were not taken. A misstep outside the magical protective circle could mean instant death for the conjurer(s), and Andras was always trying to lure them out.

The Dutch demonologist Johannes Wier, author of *Pseudomonarchia Daemonum*, says:

"Andras is a great marquesse, and is seene in an angels shape with a head like a blacke night raven, riding upon a blacke and a verie strong woolfe, flourishing with a sharpe sword in his hand, he can kill the maister, the servant, and all assistants, he is author of discords, and ruleth thirtie legions."

**Andrealphus**

Androalphus appears as the 54th demon in Johann Weyer's book, and is described as "…a great Marquis with the appearance of a Peacock who raises great noises and teaches cunning in astronomy, and when in human form also teaches geometry in a perfect manner."

Andrealphus also appears as the 65th demon in the Goetia where he is described with similar traits, but also including the ability to make men subtle in all things pertaining to Mensuration, among other things. He is also described as ruling over thirty legions and as having the ability to transform any man into a bird, and he takes the form of a peacock.

In the game *In Nomine*, Andrealphus is the Demon Prince of Lust.

## Andromalius

The Seventy-second Spirit in Order is an Earl, Great and Mighty, appearing in the Form of a man holding a big serpent in his hand. He holds a great serpent; punishes thieves, restores stolen property, and discovers all dishonest dealing.

## Astaroth

Demon of vanity and sloth, also was known as a Goddess of lust, seduction. His name is taken from that of 2nd millennium BC Phoenician goddess Astarte, an equivalent of the Babylonian Ishtar, and the earlier Sumerian Inanna. She is mentioned in the Hebrew Bible in the forms Ashtoreth (singular) and Ashtaroth (plural, in reference to multiple statues of her). This latter form was directly transliterated in the early Greek and Latin versions of the Bible, where it was less apparent that it had been a plural feminine in Hebrew.

In the Testament of Solomon, attributed to King Solomon of Israel, it, mentions Asteraoth as an angel, who is opposed to the demon of power. (cf. 1 Kings 11:4-5)

The name originally was a male demon is first known from The Book of Abramelin, written in Hebrew ca. 1458, and recurred in most occult grimoires of the following centuries. Astaroth also features as an arch-demon associated with the qliphoth according to later Kabbalistic texts.

He is depicted as a nude man with feathered wings, wearing a crown, holding a serpent in one hand, and riding a beast with dragon-like wings and a serpentine tail. According to Sebastien Michaelis he is"… a demon of the First Hierarchy, who seduces by means of laziness, vanity, and rationalized philosophies". His adversary is St. Bartholomew, who can protect against him for he has resisted Astaroth's temptations. (See *I, Lucifer: Exploring the Archtype and Origins of the Devil*, Schiffer Publishing) To others, he teaches mathematical sciences and handicrafts, can make men invisible and lead them to hidden treasures, and answers every question formulated to him. He was also said to give to mortal beings the power over serpents.

## Asmoday

According to the Goetia, " Asmoday or Asmodai is a Great King, strong and Powerful. He appeareth with three heads, whereof the first is like a Bull, the second like a Man, and the third like a Ram; he hath also the tail of a serpent and from his mouth issue flames of fire. His feet are webbed like those of a Goose. He sitteth upon an infernal Dragon, and bereth in his hand a Lance with a Banner. He is first and choicest under the Power of Amaymon, he goeth before all other.

He giveth the Ring of Virtues; he teacheth the arts of Arithmetic, Astronomy, Geometry, and all handicrafts adsolutely . He giveth true and full answers unto thy demands. He showeth the place where treasures lie, and guardeth it. He, amongst the Legions of Amaymon governeth 72 legions of Spirits inferior." kingly daimon that confers the ring of virtue; makes men invincible.

**Avnas**

Avnas takes the form of living fire; teaches & reveals secrets.

**Barbatos**

Barbatos is an Earl and Duke of Hell, ruling eighty legions of demons and has four kings as his companions to command his legions. He gives the understanding of the voices of the animals, has the power to tell the future, dispels enchantments and conciliates friends and rulers, and he can locate treasures that have been hid by magicians.

## Bathin

Bathin has under his command thirty legions of demons. He knows the virtues of precious stones and herbs, and can bring men suddenly from one country to another. His name could derive from Latin 'batha', Ethiopian (it was believed that demons could appear in the form of a black man) or from Latin 'mathios', an undetermined herb that was believed could keep serpents young. He is the demon who can who can teleport others. He is depicted as a strong man with the tail of a serpent, riding a pale horse.

## Beleth

has eighty-five legions of demons under his command. He rides a pale horse, and all kind of music is heard before him.

When he is appears as an angry man riding a horse. The conjurer must rehearse all threatens the conjurations said and then Beleth will obey and do all what he is commanded. But the conjurer must be respectful and do homage unto Beleth due to his rank, and hold a silver ring in the middle finger of the left hand against his face, as it is the use of hellish kings and princes before Amaymon.

According to *Pseudomonarchia Daemonum* Ham, Noah's son, was the first in invoking him after the flood, and wrote a book on Mathematics with his help.

**Belial**

Often identified with Satan, confusingly as both as a minion of Satan and sometimes as another name for Satan as well. His name comes from the Hebrew meaning without value. Among certain sections of the Jews, this demon was considered the chief of all the devils. He is both "the angel of lawlessness" and "the king of this world". Belial is also mentioned in the Book of Jubilees, uncircumcised heathens are considered to be "Sons of Belial".

Belial is considered the source of the seven spirits of seduction that enter men at birth, the source of impurity and lying, and the spirit of darkness. Lord of Lies is one of the Lesser Evils, part of the Great Evils of the Burning Hells.

## Berith

Berith is the god of the Canaanite city, who later came to be viewed as the demon Baalberith in Christian demonology. According to the Book of Judges, his temple was destroyed when Abimelech quelled the rising of his subjects. The name denotes a form of Ba'al-worship prevailing in Israel. The term "Ba'al" is "the God of the Covenant." The 'Covenant' and in Hebrew: refers may refer to the covenant between Israel and the people of Shechem. according to the Rabbis, with Baal-zebub, "the ba'al of flies," the god of Ekron (II Kings) He is a soldier in red with a red horse & gold crown;

He can turn metals into gold.

**Bifrons**

Earl of Hell, with twenty-six legions of demons under his command. He teaches sciences and arts to the daimon as he reveals geometry and astrology , the benefits of the gems and woods, herbs, and changes corpses from their original grave into other places, sometimes putting magick lights on the graves that seem candles. He appears as a monster, but then changes his shape into that of a man.

**Botis**

Botis is a Great President and Earl of Hell, commanding sixty legions of demons. He tells of all things past and future, and reconciles friends and foes.

He is depicted as an ugly viper, but he can changes shape to that of a human, with big teeth and two horns. He carries a sharp and bright sword in his hand. He reconciles disputes between friends and enemies

**Buer**

One of the Great Presidents of Hell, having fifty legions of demons under his command. He appears when the Sun is in Sagittarius. Buer teaches Natural and Moral Philosophy, Logic, and the nature, properties of plants, heals He also heals all infirmities, especially of men, and gives good familiars. Often depicted in the shape of

Sagittarius, which is as a centaur with a bow and arrows, or with the head of a lion and five goat legs surrounding his body to walk in every direction.

## Bune

A great Duke of Hell, Bune can summon the dead and has thirty legions of demons under his command. He changes the place of the dead and makes them demons that are under his power to gather together upon those sepulchres. Bune makes men eloquent and wise, and gives true answers to their demands and also richness. He speaks with a comely high voice, but is a daimon that assumes a monstrous form; depicted as a three-headed dragon, being his heads like those of a dog, a griffin, and a man (although according to some grimoires he has two heads like a dragon and the third like a man).

## Camio

a Great President of Hell, ruling over thirty legions of demons. Much detail is offered: He is a daimon who reveals the language of animals and of the noise of the waters too, and foretells things to come.

He is depicted in 19th and 20th century occultist illustrations as appearing in the form of the black bird called a thrush, but soon he changes his shape into a man that has a sharp sword in his hand. When answering questions he seems to stand on burning ashes or coals

## Cimeies

Cimeies also known by the alternate names Kimaris, Cimejes and Cimeries, is most widely known as the 66th daimon of the third part of the Lemegeton (popularly known as the Ars Goetia). He is described as a warrior riding a black horse, and his resume includes the ability to locate lost or hidden treasures, teach grammar, logic and rhetoric (speech). He rules over all the spirits of Africa. Much the same description is found in the earlier text of Johann Weyer's catalog of demons. Earlier still is the Munich Handbook of Necromancy: Clm 849 (published by Richard Kieckhefer, book, *Forbidden Rites: a necromancer's manual of the 15th century* lists an entity named Tuvries with much the same characteristics, except that he "has 30 legions of servitors, and can cause a person to cross seas and rivers quickly."

Aleister Crowley, in 777, gives Kimaris the Hebrew spelling KYMAVR and attributes him to the four of disks and the third decan of Capricorn by night. KYMAVR may allude to Khem-our, or black light, a form of Horus mentioned in H. P. Blavatsky's Secret Doctrine.

## Crocell

Crocell is a Great Duke of Hell that has under his command forty-eight legions of demons. He teaches geometry and all liberal sciences.

If the conjurer commands it, he will make great noises like the running of the waters and make them roar where there is none; he also warms waters and discovers baths.

Crocell is depicted as an angel that speaks mystically - teaches the mystic arts and hidden things, as well as having power over water.

## Dantalion

has many faces and changes peoples' thoughts

## Decarabia

Decarabia is also called Carabia, the is a Great Marquis of Hell, although he has no title in the hellish hierarchy in the *Pseudomonarchia Daemonum*. He has thirty legions of demons under his command.

Decarabia knows the virtues of all herbs and precious stones, and can change into all birds and sing and fly like them before the conjurer. He can appears as a star; provides birds as familiars.

**Eligos**

Abigor or Eligor), in demonology, is a Great Duke of Hell, ruling sixty legions of demons. He discovers hidden things, and knows the future, of wars, and how soldiers should meet. He also attracts the favours of lords, knights and other important persons. He is depicted as a spectre, sometimes riding a winged horse. A knight carrying a lance, an ensign and a sceptre (a serpent to some writers, especially Aleister Crowley). He is a spirit who foretells the outcome of battles.

Eligos also known as Abigor from Collin de Plancy's *Dictionnaire Infernal*

**Focalor**

A powerful Great Duke of Hell, commanding (thirty legions demons and is depicted as a man with the wings of a griffin. He summons wind and waves to drowns men, and sinks warships; but if commanded by the conjurer he will not harm anyone.

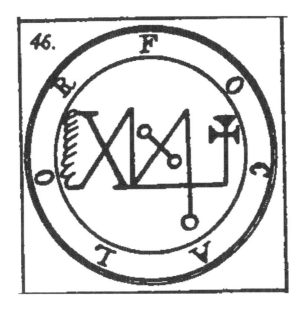

**Foras**

Is a demon who twenty-nine legions of demons. He teaches logic and ethics in all their branches, the virtues of all herbs and precious stones, can make a man witty, eloquent, invisible appears as a man, and confers longevity. As the occultist S. L. MacGregor Mathers (1904) says he is the "Thirty-first Spirit is Foras. He is a Mighty President, and appeareth in the Form of a Strong Man in Human

Shape. He can give the understanding to Men how they may know the Virtues of all Herbs and Precious Stones. He teacheth the Arts of Logic and Ethics in all their parts. If desired he maketh men invisible, and to live long, and to be eloquent. He can discover Treasures and recover things Lost. He ruleth over 29 Legions of Spirits, and his Seal is this, which wear thou, etc."

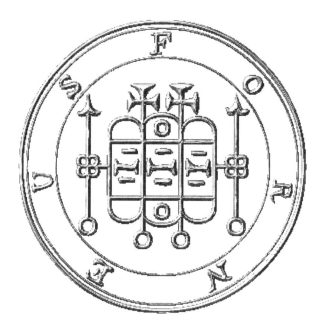

**Forneus**

This demon is fierce and depicted as a great sea monster, a Great Marquis of Hell, and has twenty-nine legions of demons under his rule. He teaches Rhetoric and languages, gives men a good name, and makes them be loved by their friends and foes.

**Furcas**

Forcas is a Knight of Hell (the rank of Knight is unique to him), and rules 20 legions of demons daimon of divination who teaches pyromancy and palmistry, as well as Philosophy, Astronomy, Astrology), Rhetoric, Logic, Chiromancy and Pyromancy. Furcas is depicted as a strong old man with white hair and long white beard, who rides a horse while holding a pitch fork, (see image).

"Furcas is a knight and commeth foorth in the similitude of a cruell man, with a long beard and a hoarie head, he sitteth on a pale horsse, carrieng in his hand a sharpe weapon, he perfectlie teacheth practike philosophie, rhetorike, logike, astronomie, chiromancie, pyromancie, and their parts: there obeie him twentie legions, " says  Johann Weyer (1583)

Image of Furcas from Collin de Plancy's *Dictionnaire Infernal*

## Gremory

Gemory, or Gomory) is a strong Duke of Hell that governs twenty-six legions of demons. He tells all things past, present and future, about hidden treasures, and procures the love of women, young and old, but especially maidens.

He is depicted as appearing in the form of a beautiful woman with the crown of a duchess tied around his waist, and riding a came . He is a divinatory daimon who reveals hidden treasure

**Gusion**

Great Duke of Hell, and rules over forty (forty-five according to other authors) legions of demons. He is depicted as a baboon he is a divinatory spirit who can answer on past, present & future, who shows the meaning of all questions that are asked to him, reconciles friends, and gives honour and dignity.

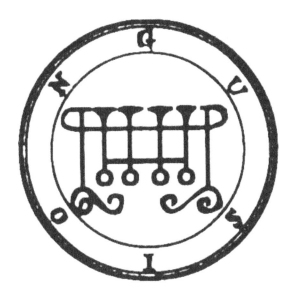

## Haagenti

A Great President of Hell, commanding thirty-three legions of demons. He makes men wise by instructing them in every subject, transmutes all metals into gold, and changes wine into water and water into wine. Haagenti is depicted as a big bull with the wings of a griffin, he is the daimon of transformation; confers wisdom.

**Halphas**

"The Thirty-eighth Spirit is Halphas, or Malthous (or Malthas). He is a Great Earl, and appeareth in the Form of a Stock-Dove. He speaketh with a hoarse Voice. His Office is to build up Towers, and to furnish them with Ammunition and Weapons, and to send Men-of-War to places appointed. He ruleth over 26 Legions of Spirits." MacGregor Mathers (1904) Halphas is a martial daimon who provides weapons and builds towers

## Haures

Haures appears in the form of a leopard; and he commands fire.

**Ipos**

Is the demon/angel with a lion-headed who makes men witty and bold.

**Kimaris**

A daimon that reveals the location of lost & hidden things.

**Glasya Labolas**

From Mathers, again, (1904) "The Twenty-fifth Spirit is Glasya-Labolas. He is a Mighty President and Earl, and showeth himself in the form of a Dog with Wings like a Gryphon. He teacheth all Arts and Sciences in an instant, and is an Author of Bloodshed and Manslaughter. He teacheth all things Past, and to Come. If desired he causeth the love both of Friends and of Foes. He can make a Man to go Invisible. And he hath under his command 36 Legions of Spirits." Demon of the spirit of strife; appears as a dog with gryphon's wings.

**Leraie**

Lerajie, a powerful marquis, who appears as an archer in a green tunic, armed with bow & arrows. He stirs up battles among men & takes a special interest in arrow wounds - which he causes to putrefy.

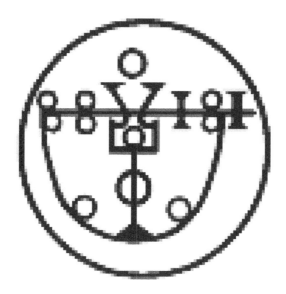

**Malphas**

A mighty Prince to some authors of Hell, having forty legions of demons under his command. He builds houses, high towers and strongholds, throws down the buildings of the enemies, can destroy the enemies' desires or thoughts and he gives good familiars, and can bring quickly artificers together from all places of the world. He accepts willingly and kindly any sacrifice offered to him, but then he will deceive the conjurer.

He is depicted as a crow that after a while or under request changes shape into a man, and speaks with a hoarse voice a martial daimon who reveals the secrets of the enemy.

## Marax

The commander of thirty-two legions of demons. He teaches Astronomy and all other liberal sciences, and gives good and wise familiars that know the virtues of all herbs and precious stones. This profile of the demon can be seen in *Pseudomonarchia Daemonum* (Johann Weyer, 1577) as well as in *Goetia* (S.L. MacGregor Mathers, 1904). A demon in the form of a bull with a man's face that reveals the secrets of stones and of the stars.

## Marbas

The fifth Spirit is Marbas. He is a Great President, and appeareth at first in the form of a Great Lion. He is the revealer of secrets; curer and causer of diseases.

## Marchosias

is a powerful Great Marquis of Hell, commanding thirty legions of demons. He is a strong and excellent fighter and very reliable to the conjurer, giving true answers to all questions. Marchosias hoped after one thousand and two hundred years to return to heaven with the non-fallen angels, but he is deceived in that hope. He is a fire-breathing winged wolf with a serpent's tail; and an excellent fighter.

**Murmur**

Great Duke and Earl of Hell, and has thirty legions of demons under his command. He teaches Philosophy, and can oblige the souls of the deceased to appear before the conjurer to answer every desired question.

Murmur is depicted as a soldier riding a Vulture or a Griffin, and wearing a ducal crown. Two of his ministers go before him making the sound of trumpets. 'Murmur' in Latin means noise, whisper, murmur, and the sound of the trumpet. Some authors portray him simply as a vulture, he is a daimon of necromancy who can retrieve the spirits of the dead.

**Naberius**

The most valiant Marquis of Hell, and has nineteen legions of demons under his command. He makes men cunning in all arts (and sciences, according to most authors), but especially in rhetoric, speaking with a hoarse voice. He also restores lost dignities and honors, although to Johann Weyer he is also Cerberus. He is considered a spirit of cunning who appears as a black crane.

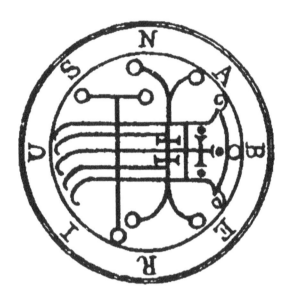

**Naphula**

Sixtieth Spirit is Vapula, or Naphula. He is a Duke Great, Mighty, and Strong; appearing in the Form of a. Lion with Gryphon's Wings. His Office is to make Men Knowing in all Handcrafts and Professions, also in Philosophy, and other Sciences. He governeth 36 Legions of Spirits, and his Seal or Character is thus made, and thou shalt wear it as aforesaid, etc daimon that appears as a winged lion; teaches craftsmanship.

**Oriax**

Oriax) is a Great Marquis of Hell, and has thirty legions of demons under his command. He knows and teaches the virtues of the stars and reveals knowledge of the planets (depending on the astrological sign in which it is in a specific moment and the influence of that sign on an individual depending on how the zodiac was configured at the moment of his/her birth) or at the moment of asking a question to the astrologist); he also gives dignities, prelacies, and the favour of friends and foes, and can metamorphose a man into any shape.. He appears as a lion with a serpent's tail.

**Orobas**

A powerful Great Prince of Hell, having twenty legions of demons under his control. He supposedly gives true answers of things past, present and to come, divinity, and the creation of the world; he also confers dignities and prelacies, and the favour of friends and foes. Orobas is faithful to the conjurer, does not permit that any spirit tempts him, and never deceives anyone. He is depicted as a horse that changes into a man under the conjurer's request.

**Ose**

Great President of Hell, ruling three legions of demons (thirty to other authors, and Pseudomonarchia Daemonum gives no number of legions). He makes men wise in all liberal sciences and gives true answers concerning divine and secret things; he also brings insanity to any person the conjurer wishes, making him/her believe that he/she is the creature or thing the magician desired. Ose is depicted as a leopard that can change the shape of men.

**Paimon**

Paimon has two hundred (legions of demons under his rule, and is more obedient to Lucifer than other kings. He has a great voice and roars as soon as he comes, speaking in this manner for a while, until the conjurer compels him and then he answers clearly the questions he is asked. When the conjurer invokes this demon he must look towards the northwest (the west to other authors), for there is where he has his house, and when Paimon appears he must be allowed to ask what he wishes and be answered, in order to obtain the same from him. Paimon teaches all arts, philosophy and sciences, and secret things; he can reveal all mysteries of the Earth, wind and water.

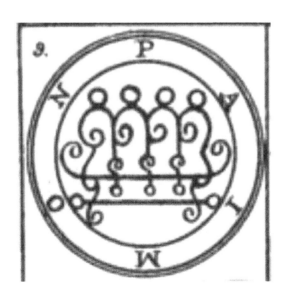

**Raum**

Mathers, (1904) "The Fortieth Spirit is Raum. He is a Great Earl; and appeareth at first in the Form of a Crow, but after the Command of the Exorcist he putteth on Human Shape. His office is to steal Treasures out King's Houses, and to carry it whither he is commanded, and to destroy Cities and Dignities of Men, and to tell all things, Past and What Is, and what Will Be; and to cause Love between Friends and Foes. He was of the Order of Thrones. He governeth 30 Legions of Spirits; and his Seal is this, which wear thou as aforesaid." Raum is a martial daimon, takes the form of a crow; destroys cities

**Ronove**

A Marquis and Great Earl of Hell, commanding twenty legions of demons. He teaches Rhetoric, languages, and gives good and loyal servants and the favour of friends and foes. He is depicted as a monster holding a staff, without detailing his appearance. He is also described as taker of old souls; often coming to earth to harvest souls of decrepit humans and animals near death.

**Sabnock**

Great Marquis of Hell, who has fifty legions of demons under his command. He builds high towers, castles and cities, furnishing them with weapons, ammunition, etc., gives good familiars, and can afflict men for several days (thirty to some authors) making gangrene their wounds and sores or filling them with worms. According to other authors he can also transform men in stone. He is lion-headed soldier; curses wounds to become diseased.

## Sallos

Great Duke of Hell, ruling thirty legions of demons (Weyer does not mention anything concerning legions under his command). He is of a pacific nature, and assists in sex magick by causeing men to love women and women to love men.

He is depicted as a gallant and handsome soldier, wearing a ducal crown, and riding a crocodile.

## Samigina

Great Marquis of Hell who rules over thirty legions of demons. He teaches all liberal sciences and gives an account of the souls of those who died in sin, and summons the souls of the drowned, speaking with a rough voice. He also answers what is asked about, and stays with the conjurer until he or she is satisfied herald of death.

## Seere

The Seventieth Spirit is Seere, Sear, or Seir. He is a Mighty Prince, and Powerful, under AMAYMON, King of the East, depicted as a man who appears on a winged horse; a messenger who transports things.

**Shax**

Great Marquis of Hell, and has power over thirty legions of demons. He takes away the sight, hearing and understanding of any person under the conjurer's request, and steals money out of kings' houses, carrying it back in 1200 years. He also steals horses and everything the conjurer asks. Shax can also discover hidden things if they are not kept by evil spirits, and sometimes gives good familiars, but sometimes those familiars deceive the conjurer. Shax is thought to be faithful and obedient, but is a great liar and will deceive the conjurer unless obliged to enter a magic triangle drawn on the floor. He will then speak marvellously and tell the truth.can render an enemy deaf, dumb, and blind.

**Sitri**

daimon that appears as a winged leopard; causes love & nakedness

**Stolas**

reigns over sixty legions of demons. He causes men to love women and vice versa, and makes them to show themselves naked if it is desired. He also reveals secrets of women, mocking them.

He is depicted with the face of a leopard and the wings of a griffin, but under the conjurer's request he changes into a very beautiful man, or as the .spirit that appears as a raven; teaches the properties of stones and stars

**Uval**

Angel, fallen, who assists in divination and love spells.

**Valefor**

Valefar is a Duke of Hell who tempts people to steal and is in charge of a good relationship among thieves. Valefar is considered a good familiar by his associates "till they are caught in the trap."as told by Waite, Arthur Edward (1913), *The Book of Ceremonial Magic*. He commands ten legions of demonsteacher of thieves who appears as a lion

**Vassago**

Vassago is a mighty Prince of Hell, ruling over twenty-six legions of demons. He tells about happenings past and future, discovers hidden and lost things, and has a good nature. He appears as an old man on a crocodile; tells past, present & future; finds hidden things.

## Vepar

a sea daimon; takes the form of a mermaid who guides ships, calms storms.

## Volac

"Valac is a great president, and commeth abroad with angels wings like a boie, riding on a twoheaded dragon, he perfectlie answereth of treasure hidden, and where serpents may be seene, which he delivereth into the conjurors hands, void of anie force or strength, and hath dominion over thirtie legions of divels." (Scot, *Discoverie of Witchcraft*) A demon that takes the form of a winged child; reveals serpents to the summoner.

**Zagan**

A Great King and President of Hell, commanding over thirty-three legions of demons. He makes men witty; he can also turn wine into water, water into wine, and blood into wine (according to *Pseudomonarchia Daemonum* blood into oil, oil into blood, and a fool into a wise man). According to other demonologists this demon is the protector of those who commit fraud with false money, and can also change copper into gold and lead into silver.

Zagan is depicted as a griffin-winged bull that turns into a man after a while. Other authors portray him as a bull-headed man with the wings of a griffin

**Zepar**

A Great Duke of Hell, clad as a soldier in red armor. He commands 26 legions of spirits. His office is to cause women to love men, and bring them together in love. He makes women barren.

*Goetic Demons*

## Appendix: Sumerian Demons

This story is the sixteenth tablet of a series called the "Evil Demon Series." The series presents an Assyrian tale with a parallel Sumerian text. As there is an original version of the tale in Sumerian, this suggests that the legend of the seven was very ancient indeed. The following translation comes from "The Seven Evil Spirits" by R.C. Thompson, published in London in 1903.

### The Evil of the Seven

Raging storms, evil gods are they, Ruthless demons, who in heaven's vault were created, are they, Workers of evil are they, They lift up the head to evil, every day to evil Destruction to work.

Of these seven the first is the South wind...

The second is a dragon, whose mouth is opened [...] That none can measure.

The third is a grim leopard, which carries off the young.

The fourth is a terrible Shibbu ...

The fifth is a furious Wolf, who knoweth not to flee,

The sixth is a rampant [...] marching against god and king.

The seventh is a storm, an evil wind, which takes vengeance.

Seven are they, messengers to King Anu are they,

From city to city darkness work they,

A hurricane, which mightily hunts in the heavens, are they

Thick clouds, that bring darkness in heaven, are they,

Gusts of wind rising, which cast gloom over the bright day,

With the Imkhullu, the evil wind, forcing their way, are they,

The overflowing of Adad mighty destroyers, are they, At the right of Adad stalking, are they, In the height of heaven, like lightning flashing, are they, To wreak destruction forward go they, In the broad heaven, the home of Anu, the King, evilly do they arise, and none to oppose.

## The Seven in the *Enuma Elish*

The description of the Seven is also echoed in the *Enuma Elish*, the Mesopotamian creation myth. The Seven attack the moon god Sin, causing his light to go dim in the heavens. The other gods take note and send the mighty Marduk to save the day. Before he meets with them in battle, the following lines are given to describe them:

I.

Destructive storms and evil winds are they, A storm of evil, presaging the baneful storm, A storm of evil, forerunner of the baneful storm. Mighty children, mighty sons are they, Messengers of Namtar are they, Throne-bearers of Ereshkigal. The flood driving through the land are they. Seven gods of the wide heavens, Seven gods of the broad earth, Seven robber-gods are they. Seven gods of universal sway, Seven evil gods, Seven evil demons, Seven evil and violent demons, Seven in heaven, seven on earth.

## II

Neither male nor female are they. Destructive whirlwinds they, Having neither wife nor offspring. Compassion and mercy they do not know. Prayer and supplication they do not hear. Horses reared in the mountains, Hostile to Ea. Throne-bearers of the gods are they.

Standing on the highway, befouling the street. Evil are they, evil are they, Seven they are, seven they are, Twice seven they are.

## III

The high enclosures, the broad enclosures like a flood they pass through. From house to house they dash along. No door can shut them out, No bolt can turn them back. Through the door, like a snake, they glide, Through the hinge, like the wind, they storm. Tearing the wife from the embrace of the man, Snatching the child from the knees of a man, Driving the freedman from his family home.

## A Charm Against the Seven Evil Spirits

Seven are they, seven are they! In the channel of the deep seven are they! In the radiance of heaven seven are they! In the channel of the deep in a palace grew they up. Male they are not, female they are not. In the midst of the deep are their paths.

Wife they have not, son they have not. Order and kindness know they not. Prayer and supplication hear they not. The cavern in the mountain they enter.

Unto Ea are they hostile. The throne-bearers of the gods are they. Disturbing the lily in the torrents are they set. Baleful are they, baleful are they. Seven are they, seven are they, seven twice again are they.

May the spirits of heaven remember, may the spirits of earth remember.

# 𝕬𝖋𝖙𝖊𝖗𝖜𝖔𝖗𝖉

The spirit world, and all the inhabitants thought to reside in Heaven and Hell have a strong vibration of energy to them even in merely a mental thought. Devout worshippers of either path may call upon the aid of Angels or Demonic forces to work their magic. Whether one believes in these forces is irrelevant in the end, for if the Will of the sorcerer is strong enough so shall it be done! I hope you have enjoyed this work by Lucien as much as I have in putting it into reality with him. There is no limited to what mankind can explore, so long as he remains true to himself and use the wisdom of Soloman to lead a life full of promise for a better tomorrow.

*Goetic Demons*

# 𝔅𝔦𝔟𝔩𝔦𝔬𝔤𝔯𝔞𝔭𝔥𝔶

Belanger, Michelle. *The Dictionary of Demons: Names of the Damned.* Llewellyn, 2010.

Davidson, Gustav. *A Dictionary of Angels.* The Free Press, New York: 1971

Mathers, S.L. MacGregor. *The Book of the Sacred Magic of Abramelin the Mage.* Dover Publications, New York: 1975

Mathers, S. L. MacGregor. The Key of Solomon the King. Samuel Weiser, Maine: 1972.

Mathers, S.L. MacGregor. *The Goetia: the Lesser Key of Solomon the King.* Samuel Weiser, Maine: 1995.

Mathers, S.L. MacGregor. *The Grimoire of Armadel.* Samuel Weiser, Maine: 1995

Nocturnum, Corvis. *Satan's Minions: Fallen Angels and other dark creatures* Dark Moon Press, Indiana, 2011

Savedow, Steve. *Goetic Evocation: the Magician's Workbook vol. 2.* Eschaton Productions, Chicago: 1996.

*The Sixth and Seventh Books of Moses.* Egyptian Press. circa 1890.

Made in the USA
Monee, IL
10 August 2022

11335105R00056